A LOOK AT MONEY MATTERS

STOCKS

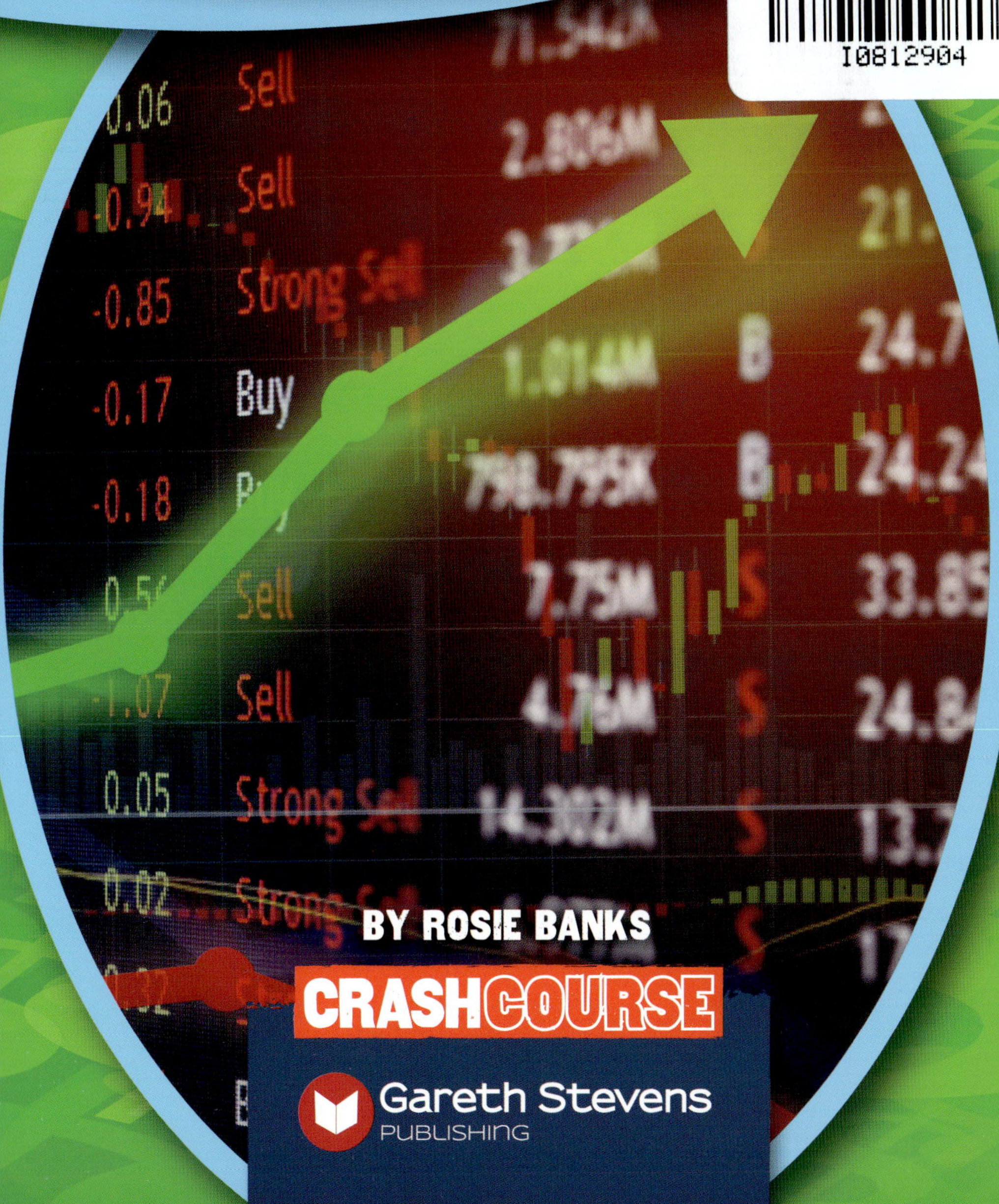

BY ROSIE BANKS

CRASHCOURSE

Gareth Stevens PUBLISHING

Please visit our website, www.garethstevens.com. For a free color catalog of all our high-quality books, call toll free 1-800-542-2595 or fax 1-877-542-2596.

Library of Congress Cataloging-in-Publication Data
Names: Banks, Rosie (Children's fiction writer), author.
Title: Stocks / Rosie Banks.
Description: Buffalo : Gareth Stevens Publishing, [2024] | Series: A look at money matters | Includes index.
Identifiers: LCCN 2023031951 (print) | LCCN 2023031952 (ebook) | ISBN 9781538292372 (library binding) | ISBN 9781538292365 (paperback) | ISBN 9781538292389 (ebook)
Subjects: LCSH: Stocks--Juvenile literature. | Securities--Juvenile literature. | Investments--Juvenile literature. | Capital market--Juvenile literature.
Classification: LCC HG4661 .B365 2024 (print) | LCC HG4661 (ebook) | DDC 332.63/228--dc23/eng/20230710
LC record available at https://lccn.loc.gov/2023031951
LC ebook record available at https://lccn.loc.gov/2023031952

First Edition

Published in 2024 by
Gareth Stevens Publishing
2544 Clinton Street
Buffalo, NY 14224

Designer: Leslie Taylor
Editor: Therese Shea

Photo credits: Cover (image) Travis Wolfe/Shutterstock.com; cover & series art (background) creativenv/Shutterstock.com; series art (falling coins) Absent Vector/Shutterstock.com, (moneybag) VectorArtist7/Shutterstock.com; p. 5 Dean Drobot/Shutterstock.com; p. 7 ARMMY PICCA/Shutterstock.com; p. 9 U.S. Bureau of Engraving and Printing; Restoration and imaging by Gwillhickers/https://commons.wikimedia.org/wiki/File:Argonaut_Oil_%26_Mining_Co_stock_1900_and_rev_stamps.jpg; p. 11 1st footage/Shutterstock.com; p. 13 Sorn340 Studio Images/Shutterstock.com; p. 15 Javen/Shutterstock.com; p. 17 orhan akkurt/Shutterstock.com; p. 19 lev radin/Shutterstock.com; p. 21 dennizn/Shutterstock.com; p. 23 Gorodenkoff/Shutterstock.com; p. 25 Everett Collection/Shutterstock.com; p. 27 (inset) trabantos/Shutterstock.com, (nyc bull) emin kuliyev/Shutterstock.com; p. 29 Daniel Myjones/Shutterstock.com.

Printed in the United States of America

CPSIA compliance information: Batch #CW24GS: For further information contact Gareth Stevens at 1-800-542-2595.

CONTENTS

Words in the glossary appear in **bold** type the first time they are used in the text.

TAKING STOCK

Do you have a store you love to go to? Maybe it's a bookstore or a candy shop in your neighborhood. Imagine owning or partly owning that business. You might be able to! Some businesses sell ownership, or stock, in their company.

MAKE THE GRADE

Stock represents, or stands for, ownership in a company.

WHY BUY STOCK?

Stock is an investment in a company. An investment is something people buy hoping it will gain more value. They hope the stock's value will increase, or go up. Then they can sell their stock for more money than they bought it for.

MAKE THE GRADE

People use investments to build wealth, or money. Stocks are one way to do this.

SHARES OF STOCK

A share is a piece of stock. A person who owns shares is a shareholder. A company sells a certain number of shares. This is called issuing stock. Each share costs an amount of money. The more shares a shareholder has, the more ownership they have.

MAKE THE GRADE

Companies once gave stock certificates, or official papers, like this to shareholders. They now keep records on computers.

Shareholders share in a company's **profits**. When the company becomes more successful, its share prices go up. So, the shareholder's stock is worth more. However, share prices can go down too. This is a **risk** of owning stocks.

MAKE THE GRADE

Some kinds of stock pay dividends. These are payments a company makes to the shareholder at certain times.

BUY
SELL

WHY COMPANIES SELL STOCK

Not every business sells stock. It's a way to raise money, though. The money businesses make from issuing stock is called capital. The capital can pay off **debt**, make the company larger, or help make a new **product**.

MAKE THE GRADE

Businesses give some power to shareholders. Shareholders can vote on some company **decisions**.

GOING PUBLIC

When a large company decides to issue stock for the first time, it may join, or come together with, others in a stock market, or stock exchange. It has an initial, or first, public offering of its shares. This is also called an IPO.

MAKE THE GRADE

Companies that don't meet a stock exchange's rules can still sell stock. They can sell shares in over-the-counter (OTC) markets. These shares are often less money.

Many countries have one or more stock exchanges. The New York Stock Exchange (NYSE) is one of the most famous. Stock exchanges were once places where buyers and sellers did all their work. Much work takes place online now.

MAKE THE GRADE

You can't go the NYSE to buy stock. People called floor brokers represent most buyers and sellers. They buy and sell for their **clients**.

PM
LISTED
NYSE
GTS
NYSE
GTS
EXCHANGE

At the IPO, the shares are sold to the public for the first time. The new shareholders can then sell and buy the shares using the stock exchange. This is called trading. The price of shares can change a lot in a day.

MAKE THE GRADE

Businesses that sell stock go from being a **private** business to a public business. In the picture on the next page, a sign announces Facebook's IPO in 2012.

NASDAQ WELCOMES
FACEBOOK
NASDAQ LISTED [FB]
MAY 18, 2012
facebook
NASDAQ
MAX PAYNE
MAY 15
FB NASDAQ LISTED
MAY 18, 2012
facebook
NASDAQ LISTED
MAY 18, 2012

CHECK THE CHART

A company in a stock exchange is known by its stock **symbol**. For example, the Apple company's symbol is AAPL. People interested in trading look at a company's stock chart. It lists the cost of each share and how much the cost has changed over time.

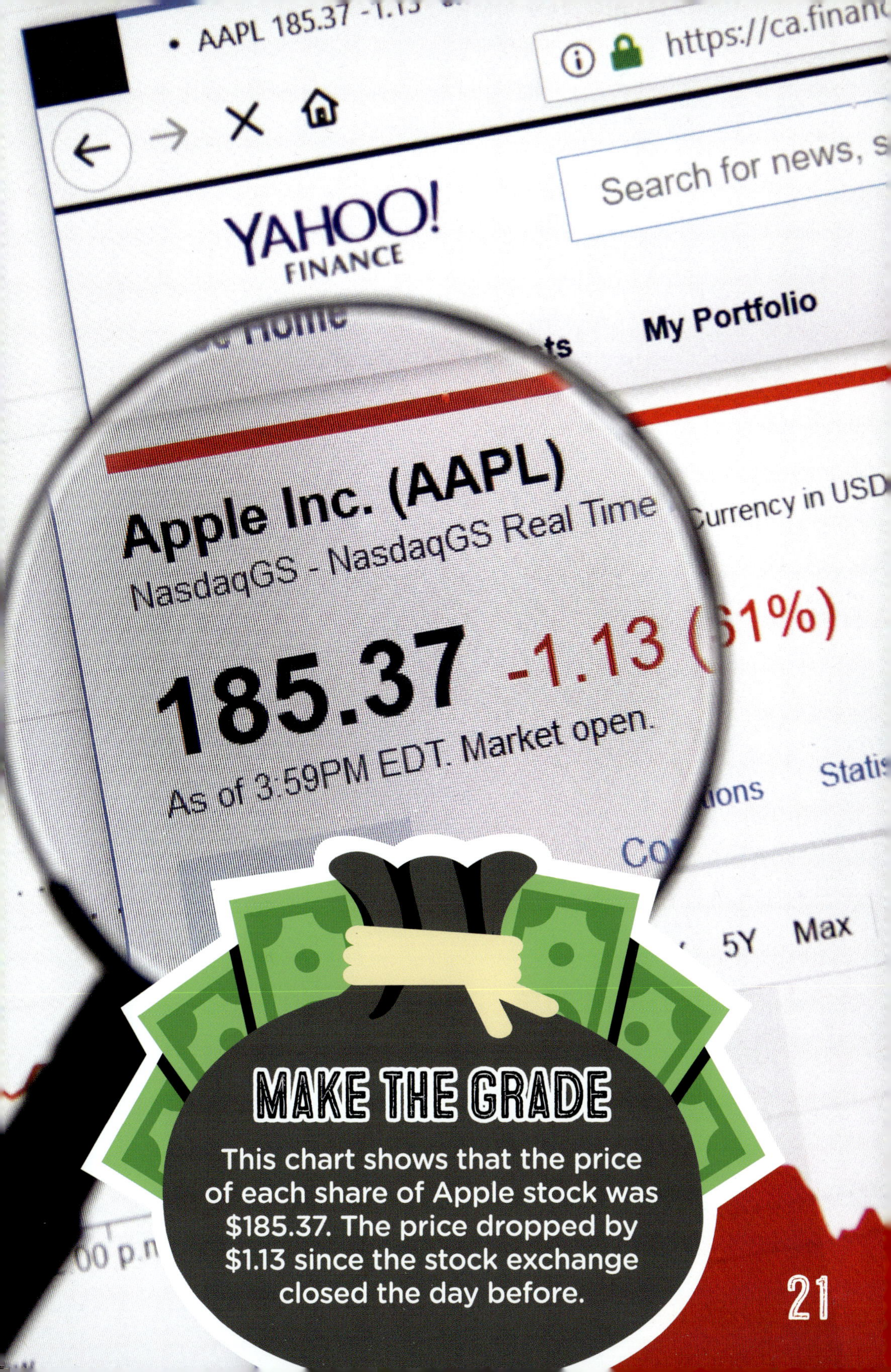

MAKE THE GRADE

This chart shows that the price of each share of Apple stock was $185.37. The price dropped by $1.13 since the stock exchange closed the day before.

UPS AND DOWNS

Why do a company's share prices go down? It could be because of something at the company or outside it. Maybe the company's product didn't work or didn't sell well. A bad **economy**, a war, and fear about the future can make prices drop too.

MAKE THE GRADE

A successful company and a good economy can make stock prices go up. People buy shares if they think they'll increase in value.

THE GREAT CRASH

When stock market values drop sharply, it's called a crash. A terrible crash happened in the United States in the 1920s. Prices had been climbing for several years. Then they began to fall in October 1929. Most shareholders tried to sell. Some stocks became worthless.

MAKE THE GRADE

Many people lost their money in the Great Crash of 1929. It was one of the causes of the **Great Depression**. In this picture, people out of work during the Depression wait for bread.

BULLS AND BEARS

When stock market prices rise for months, it's called a bull market. When prices go down for months, it's called a bear market. Bear markets are often shorter than bull markets. Bull and bear markets are an expected part of investing.

MAKE THE GRADE

These bull and bear figures are outside the stock exchange in Frankfurt, Germany. New York City also has a bull statue in its **financial** district, or neighborhood, shown below.

YOUR FINANCIAL FUTURE

In most states, people must wait until they're 18 to buy stock. However, you can prepare now if stocks interest you. Listen to stock market news. Watch share prices of the companies you like. You'll learn a lot about the risks and **rewards** of investing.

MAKE THE GRADE

Many people use stocks to make money for **retirement**. As they get close to retiring, they make sure they don't have stock in risky companies.

FIVE LARGEST STOCK EXCHANGES (IN JANUARY 2023)

Name	**Country**	**Total Value of Companies' Shares**
New York Stock Exchange (NYSE)	United States	$22.6 **trillion**
National Association of Securities Dealers Automated Quotations (NASDAQ)	United States	$18 trillion
Shanghai Stock Exchange (SSE)	China	$7.2 trillion
European New Exchange Technology (EURONEXT)	Europe	$6.6 trillion
Japan Exchange Group, Inc. (JPX)	Japan	$5.6 trillion

GLOSSARY

client: Someone who pays another person for a service.

debt: An amount of money owed.

decision: A choice made after thinking about a matter.

economy: The money made in an area and how it is made.

financial: Having to do with money.

Great Depression: A period of economic troubles with widespread unemployment and poverty (1929–1939).

private: Owned by one person or a group and not by the public.

product: Something made that is offered for sale.

profit: The money made in a business or through investing after costs are paid.

retirement: The time period of a person's life after they stop working.

reward: Money or other payment offered in return for something.

risk: A chance that something bad will happen.

symbol: A picture, shape, object, or other representation of something.

trillion: The number 1,000,000,000,000.

FOR MORE INFORMATION

BOOKS

Brezina, Corona, and Barbara Gottfried. *What You Need to Know About Stocks*. New York, NY: Rosen Publishing, 2020.

Fernandes, Bonnie J. *The Value of Stocks, Bonds, and Investments*. San Diego, CA: ReferencePoint Press, 2021.

WEBSITE

Stock Exchange

kids.britannica.com/kids/article/stock-exchange/353812

Read more about stock exchanges and how they work.

Publisher's note to educators and parents: Our editors have carefully reviewed these websites to ensure that they are suitable for students. Many websites change frequently, however, and we cannot guarantee that a site's future contents will continue to meet our high standards of quality and educational value. Be advised that students should be closely supervised whenever they access the internet.

INDEX